Souvenir Booklet of the Maryland Eastern Shore

Short sketches of the origins
of more than 150 towns and locations

DISCOVER WHY IT'S CALLED . . .

by
Dex Nilsson

Illustrations by Jon Haislip

Map Sketches by Dex Nilsson

Twinbrook Communications
Rockville, MD

Single copies may be purchased directly from Twinbrook Communications, P.O. Box 730, Twinbrook Station, Rockville, MD 20848-0730. Enclose check for $5.95 plus $1.35 handling and shipping. Retailers, libraries, distributors, and similar organizations should request standard discount schedule.

Library of Congress Catalog Card Number: 91-65521

ISBN 0-9629170-0-1

ABOUT THIS BOOKLET

This booklet is written for folks who visit or live on the Maryland Eastern Shore and Delmarva Penisula. And who wonder about the names, and how towns got started, and what happened in these places many years ago.

This is the first booklet with this information that is arranged for people riding through the Eastern Shore. The booklet is arranged by county, starting as one goes east across the Chesapeake Bay Bridge. Each county chapter begins with a map, showing the most commonly traveled routes and approximate locations of the places described.

There are more scholarly books on the subject. My goal has been to present the essence of Maryland history and key biographical sketches in an easily accessible manner and hopefully readable form, for folks who want a little information but mainly want what is called "a quick read." More likely, some trip information, vacation reading, or a souvenir to take home.

Economics has forced decisions about content. Many stories – like those about Gary Cooper's first feature film made near Easton, or how Annie Oakley liked the Choptank so much she and Frank Butler settled in Cambridge for a while – couldn't be included. Thus, this booklet is by no means all–encompassing.

I've cited at the end of the booklet some of the published source material I used. In addition, I visited each county, its courthouse, its main library. I traveled to nearly every city mentioned. Additional sources were magazines, newspaper articles, maps, and of course, on–site conversations. Of significance were the Maryland history collection in the Montgomery County Library at Rockville and files of the Library of Maryland History, Maryland Historical Society, Baltimore.

A word about the names themselves: Because Maryland was such an early English settlement (third, behind Jamestown and Plymouth) in America, most Eastern Shore names are from the Indian (e.g., Chesapeake) or are transfers from other English sites (Salisbury). Many are named for a person (Crisfield). Others, to a lesser degree, are locational (Easton), descriptive (Ocean City), inspirational (Harmony), coined (Marydel), or derived from incidents (Royal Oak).

And so, read on – perhaps as you ride along – and discover some fascinating Maryland history.

TABLE OF CONTENTS

QUEEN ANNE'S COUNTY

QUEEN ANNE'S COUNTY, properly written with the *'s*, was established in 1706, four years after the queen took the throne as Queen of England, Scotland, and Ireland. The daughter of James II and his first wife, Anne Hyde, she ruled 1702–14, bringing political calm to England for the first time in 75 years, and by doing so, achieving a measure of popularity from all sides.

The 17 Queen Anne's locations described in this chapter are sequenced from the Bay Bridge northeast following U.S. 301.

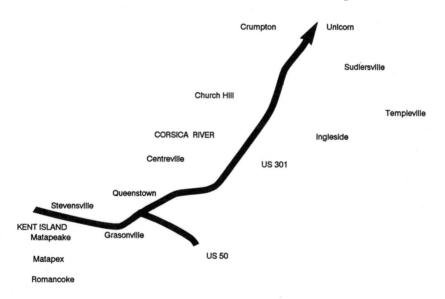

CHESAPEAKE BAY. Chesapeake comes from an Indian word and means the "Great Shell–Fish Bay." Captain John Smith explored Chesapeake Bay in 1608. He went all the way to the Susquehanna, but didn't identify the Wye or Chester rivers, and made virtually no mention of Kent Island.

KENT ISLAND is the first approach from the west to the Eastern Shore, at the east end of the Bay Bridge.

The island was settled by traders and adventurers from Virginia – first by William Claiborne, son of Sir Edward Claiborne of Westmoreland, England. William came to Virginia in 1621 as "a gentleman adventurer" to survey and map. By 1624 he was a member of the Governor's Council, and by 1625, Secretary of State for Virginia, a post he held 1626–37 and 1652–60. Initially, he was granted permission to explore Chesapeake Bay and given a license to trade with the Indians. In 1628, he received a special commission to employ men and ships. There is no question that by 1631 – and likely even in the 1620s – as a Virginian, he had established a trading post on what is now Kent Island.

But in 1632, King Charles made a grant to George Calvert, first Lord Baltimore, of territory north of Virginia and on both sides of the Chesapeake Bay, including the whole of the peninsula on the eastern shore (and extending to the western shore, from the 40th degree of north latitude down to the mouth of the Potomac River, and westwardly to the river's source).

Instead of agreeing to the Calvert claim and giving up his lands in Maryland, Claiborne fought it both literally and figuratively, in the New World and in England for almost half a century.

For example, at one point, Claiborne sent his pinnace, *Long Tayle*, to the Patuxent River to trade, an act of defiance of Lord Baltimore's territory. The vessel was seized by members of Calvert's group. Claiborne then sent the *Cockatrice*, with 13 armed men, to demand the return of the *Long Tayle*. Calvert in turn outfitted the *St. Margaret* and the *St. Helen*, and the hostile ships met in Pocomoke Sound, April 25, 1635, in the first naval engagement ever held in American waters. Three Kent Islanders were killed, three others wounded; one Marylander was killed.

In 1637, while Claiborne was in England, agents of Lord Baltimore seized Kent Island, and Baltimore's claim was later confirmed by the king. But, during the English Civil War, Claiborne supported Parliament. In 1651, he was appointed to a commission to bring Virginia to accept Parliamentary supremacy, and he

seized control of Maryland for Parliament. However, the resto-
ration of Charles II in 1660 brought final reversal to Claiborne's
own fortunes. He never again got to visit his Isle of Kent. As late
as 1677, when he was 90 years old, he made one last attempt to
have title restored and wrote to Charles II. He died before there
was an answer.

For all the Virginian's losses in retaining rights to permanent interests in Maryland, he is undoubtedly the one who gave the island its name, from the English county of Kent, which had been
his home before his adventures in America.

STEVENSVILLE, first town at the base of the east end of the Bay
Bridge, is on or close to the town of Broad Creek, and is thus the
oldest settlement within the county. Apparently it was named for
Samuel Stevens, Maryland's 20th governor (1823–25), who was
born and died on the Eastern Shore.

ROMANCOKE, at the southern end of Kent Island, was the
name of William Claiborne's plantation on Kent Island. He used
the same name in Virginia, where he was known as Claiborne of
Romancoke. Dependent upon which Indian derivation you may

Romancoke

prefer, the name means circling waters or where there is low–ly-
ing ground. The name was also given to a ferry that ran between
Romancoke and Claiborne, a town across Eastern Bay in Talbot
County, west of St. Michaels. That ferry ran until 1952.

MATAPEAKE and **MATAPEX** lie on the first road south from the base of the Bay Bridge. Matapeake was the name of the Chesapeake Bay ferry that ran from Sandy Point to Kent Island. Matapex is 4 miles further south, and takes its name from a private brick house believed to have been built in the 1600s. However, all these names derive from the Matapeake Indians of Kent Island, whose name means "expanse of water" or "junction of waters."

KENT ISLAND NARROWS. Narrow is a nautical term meaning strait connecting two bodies of water. In this case, the strait separates Kent Island from the mainland and connects the mouth of the Chester River on the north to Prospect Bay and the Miles River on the south. The word narrows is almost always used plural, for no apparent reason.

GRASONVILLE, about 9 miles from the eastern end of the Bay Bridge, was named for William Grason (1786–1868), who was born in Queen Anne's County, was called "the Queen Anne Farmer," and served as Maryland's 28th governor.

CORSICA RIVER flows from Centreville to the Chester River to Chesapeake Bay. The De Courcey family in America originated in Calvert County. In 1658, the second Lord Baltimore granted to Colonel Henry Coursey "Coursys Lords Gift" or the "Thumb Grant" – as much land as the space he could cover on a map with his thumb. In 1660 he moved there, to Queen Anne's County.

John and William Coursey, the younger sons, gave their name to Coursey's Creek (now Queenstown Creek) that flows past Queenstown to the Chester River, and to the neck of land between Queenstown Creek and the Wye River. You may know that neck better as the land on which Highways 50 and 301 intersect. Apparently Corsica, Corsica Neck, Coursey Point, Decoursey Road, De Courcy Island are all variations of the family name.

The Corsica was always known as Corsica Creek. What suddenly made it a river was a legislative act in 1886.

QUEENSTOWN, to the left of the U.S. 50 and 301 intersection, was named in 1707 Queenstown or Queen Anne's Town, and during the mid–1700s served as seat of Queen Anne's County.

CENTREVILLE. Seat of Queen Anne's County. Originally Chester Mills, Old Chester Mill, and Old Chester Church, Centreville stems from post–Revolutionary times.

The original county seat was at Queenstown, but in 1782 the legislature authorized the sale of the courthouse and jail at Queenstown and the construction of new buildings more centrally located at the head of the Corsica River. The courthouse was completed in 1792, the town laid out in 1794, and the current name adopted in 1797. The courthouse is still in use today, and is the oldest courthouse in continuous use in Maryland.

Maryland has Centervilles in Charles, Frederick, Prince Georges, Somerset, and Washington counties, so named probably because they were in the center of a region or county. However, it is said Centreville adopted the French "re" spelling to recognize French aid received during the Revolution.

Charles Willson Peale was born in 1741 near Centreville. His father had been master at schools in Centreville and Chesterton. Charles is best known for the first painting of George Washington, whom he eventually painted 60 times. In his later years, while making drawings of mammoth bones, he conceived the idea of founding an institution for the respository of his natural curiosities and paintings, which led to the Philadelphia Academy of Fine Arts. Charles had a dozen children – Raphael, Titian, Rubens, and Rembrandt among them – with Rembrandt Peale attaining as much fame as a painter as his father.

CHURCH HILL, just 8 miles northeast of Centreville, does have a church on a hill, after which it is named. Indeed in 1887, there were three churches. The original was St. Luke's Protestant Episcopal Church, built 1732.

5

CHURCH HILL

Church Hill

INGLESIDE, 11 miles east of Centreville, is located in marshy headwaters of Tuckahoe Creek. It was originally called Long Marsh, then Beaver Dam, which became a post office in 1837. The name Ingleside is attributed to a local farm. The Powhatan Indian name for Long Marsh is Tappahannah, perhaps the only occurrence of a Maryland counterpart to the Virginia Rappahannock. They both mean "stream of the lapping waters."

TEMPLEVILLE, 20 miles northeast of Centreville, nearly on the Maryland–Deleware border, was Bullockville or Bullock Town before being Templeville. A bullock is a castrated bull, perhaps used as a beast of burden. Templeville was incorporated about 1870, and is named for the Temple family, local farmers, one of whom was sheriff of Queen Anne's County in 1869, and another Governor of Delaware. Only the north side of the main street is in Queen Anne's County. The south side is in Caroline County.

SUDLERSVILLE is 15 miles northeast of Centreville. Sudler's Cross Roads became a post office in 1811, and the name was changed to Sudlersville in 1839. The Sudler family name is found in records dating as far back as 1694.

John Franklin Baker was born in Trappe in 1886, and in the early 1900s was hitting baseballs "so far out in the cornfield that nobody could find them." With the Philadelphia Athletics from 1909–14, he led the American League four times in home runs (earning the name "Home Run" Baker), twice in RBIs, and once in doubles. By 1924, however, he had retired from 13 seasons of major league baseball and was managing the Easton Farmers in the Eastern Shore League when a Sudlersville farmer named Dell Foxx asked him to consider giving his 16–year–old son a chance to play. Son James Emory "Jimmie" Foxx did play, and so well that Baker called his old manager in Philadelphia, Connie Mack, to sign the boy. Foxx entered the major leagues when he was 18 and in a 20–year career, led the American League in home runs four times, RBIs three times, and batting average twice, connecting for 534 home runs lifetime. The Sudlersville star was inducted into the Baseball Hall of Fame in 1951. The Trappe star wasn't far behind, getting the same honor in 1955.

UNICORN is one mile southeast of Millington. A wool carding establishment, later known as Unicorn Mills, was established here in 1810.

CRUMPTON is 7 miles upstream from Chestertown. As early as 1708, McAllister's Ferry crossed the Chester River at this point. The first bridge across the river was erected here in 1865. The present name is from William Crump who "took up a large tract of land." Between 1858 and the 1870s, two New Jersey promoters tried to build a larger town here, but they failed. A map of 1877 shows about 600 lots in the town, most unoccupied. Crumpton was the point at which steamboats on the Chester River turned around. The movie *Showboat* was filmed near Crumpton.

KENT COUNTY

KENT COUNTY was, in 1642, called the Isle and County of Kent, taking its name from Kent County, England. Later, as boundaries changed, Kent Island became part of Queen Anne's County.

The 9 locations of Kent County described here can be found close to U.S. 301 going northeast, and then returning west via MD 213 and 20.

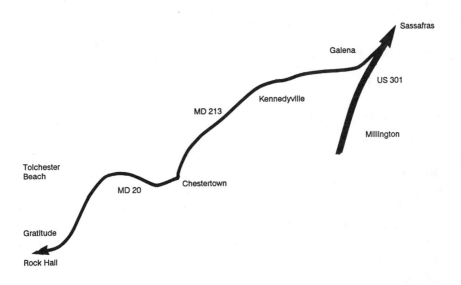

CHESTER RIVER is the dividing line between Queen Anne's and Kent counties. It was known as such as early as 1667. Its name comes from the city of Chester in Cheshire, England.

MILLINGTON was originally known as Head of Chester, where several small streams meet to form the Chester River. It is partly in Kent County, partly in Queen Anne's. A fire in 1904 destroyed most of the town, except for several houses that date from the late 1700s and early 1800s. The foundation of one mill still standing is believed to date from the 1760s. In 1819, Head of Chester became Millington, officially recognized with its post office in

1827. It is unclear whether the name stems from the many water wheel mills and a thriving woolen mill industry in the area, or from a settler named Richard Millington.

GALENA, 14 miles northeast of Chestertown, was in 1789 called Georgetown Cross Roads. Later it was Downs' Crossroads, from William Downs' tavern, built in 1763 on the water–stage route between Annapolis and Philadelphia. It burned in 1893. The present name comes from a deposit of galena, which is lead sulfide, the principal lead ore. The ore was being mined here in 1813, taken to Philadelphia, and reportedly made into "knee buckles, spoons, and casters."

SASSAFRAS is a village on the Sassafras River, in the northeast portion of the county, near the Maryland–Delaware state line. The river separates Kent County from Cecil County to its north. The river was discovered and explored by John Smith during 1607–1609. He named it Tockwough, which was the original Indian name for sassafras root, from which they made bread. Sassafras tea was popular during the 1800s. The ultimate derivation of the word sassafras, however, is unclear.

KENNEDYVILLE is a community of Amish, settled about 1954, and not named for President Kennedy. It is reportedly named for a Pennsylvania promoter who purchased the land on the main north–south road where he knew the railroad would cross it.

CHESTERTOWN, seat of Kent County. Kent has had four county seats: Fort Kent (established by William Claiborne), New Yarmouth, Olde Town or Old Town (once known as Quaker Neck Landing), and Chestertown (once known as Chester Ferry, Town–On–Chester, and New Town). The first courthouse was built in Chestertown in 1697, the town was laid out in 1706, and under the name New Town, it became a port of entry. An act of 1730 lays out "a–new" a "town" to be called "Chestertown."

Because of its location on the flourishing Chester River, it became one of Maryland's leading ports before the Revolution, and its foreign trade developed a wealthy society, some of whose homes beside the river still stand. The city was scene of the "Maryland tea party" in 1774, when tea brought into port by the brigantine *Geddes* was thrown overboard. A short time later, Chestertown sent provisions to the people of Boston, who were suffering from the effects of the Boston Port Act, and was the only Maryland city to do so.

In 1780, Rev. William Smith became rector of Chester Parish. He called a meeting of the Maryland Episcopal Church to reorganize the church that, given the Revolution, could no longer be headed by the King of England, and which then resulted in the name Episcopal for the Church of England in America. Smith was eventually nominated as bishop of Maryland, and in 1789, became provost of the University of Pennsylvania.

Rev. Smith also founded Washington College, which still operates today, in 1782. A Kent school had been established as early as 1707. The Kent County Free School was established in 1723 when the Maryland Assembly offered an endowment of 100 acres for a free school in each county. By 1782, the school had 140 pupils, and the Assembly agreed to charter it as a college if a £10,000 endowment could be raised in five years. Rev. Smith collected the money in five months, and the charter was granted. The school is considered the first free school in the U.S. and was instrumental in bringing the concept of free public education to the U.S. It was named after George Washington, with his permission – the only such institution named for him during his lifetime – and he was granted an honorary degree of Doctor of Laws from the college. So have been Presidents Roosevelt, Truman, and Eisenhower.

Some other books about the Eastern Shore mention Home Run Baker and Jimmie Foxx (see Sudlersville). Few mention a retired farmer at Chesterton named William Beck Nicholson. Bill spent 16 years in the major leagues, was voted to 4 All–Star games, led the National League in 1943 with 29 home runs and 128 RBIs, and in 1944 hit 4 consecutive home runs.

TOLCHESTER BEACH, 9 miles west of Chestertown and on the Bay, was an area of 400 acres surveyed for William Tolson in 1659. The name itself is likely a compound of Tolson and the nearby Chester River. In 1877, a resort was opened on the beach by the Tolchester Beach Improvement Company, which ultimately owned four steamers and 155 acres of land, complete with grand hotel, arcade, ferris wheel, dance floor, and race track. The resort closed in 1961, and the whole property is now private.

GRATITUDE is another town on the water. It was once called Deep Landing. The present name comes from the steamboat out of Philadelphia, the *Gratitude*, which regularly docked here.

ROCK HALL, 10 miles southwest of Chestertown, is directly across the Bay from Baltimore, yet it was of importance as early as 1708 as the terminus of a post road from the North for many years, and the point of departure for passengers for Annapolis

Rock Hall

and the South. George Washington crossed from Rock Hall many times, and Lt. Col. Tench Tilghman crossed on the Rock Hall ferry in 1781 as he was taking news of Cornwallis' surrender at Yorktown to the Continental Congress in Philadelphia. Tilghman's father is buried in Rock Hall in the cemetery of St. Paul's Episcopal Church. So is Tallulah Bankhead, the actress, whose sister lived in Rock Hall.

Some say the name was taken from Rock Haul because of large hauls of rockfish taken there, others say the town was named for Rock Hall, a mansion which stood at the landing west of town.

CAROLINE COUNTY

CAROLINE COUNTY was named after Lady Caroline Calvert, sister of Frederick, the sixth and last Lord Baltimore.

The 16 locations whose origins are described in this chapter are arranged in three parts: eastward along MD 404; eastward from Easton along MD 331, 313, and 577; and the northern portion of the county which contains no major "tourist–route" but instead centers around the north–south railroads that arose late in the last century.

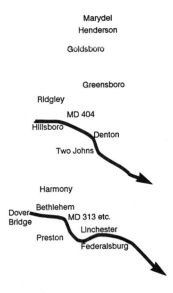

TUCKAHOE CREEK and its tributaries form much of the line between Caroline and Talbot counties. The word comes from the Indian tucka, which means a round root used as food, same as tockwough (see Sassafras River).

HILLSBORO was originally Tuckahoe Bridge, because a bridge spanned Tuckahoe Creek here as early as 1750. The present name is for Lord Hillsboro, a member of the Calvert family. The village was incorporated in 1822.

RIDGELY is a fully planned city. In 1867, several businessmen under the name Maryland and Baltimore Land Association planned a city on a site along the Maryland and Delaware Railroad near land owned by the Rev. Greenbury W. Ridgely, who held several thousand acres in the area. Rev. Ridgely already had interests in the construction of a Queenstown and Harrington Railroad, and to assure his cooperation, the businessmen agreed to name their town after him. It was surveyed, mapped, promoted, but under financed, so that by 1868 the effort failed. But the town continued to exist, and its borders are still square and its main street wide as originally laid out.

Ridgely was from Lexington, Kentucky, educated as a lawyer and a one–time law partner of Henry Clay. He later joined the ministry and held services at several churches. He's buried at Hillsboro.

GREENSBORO. In 1732, an act was passed to establish a town at the bridge near the head of the Choptank River. It was then known as Choptank Bridge or Bridge Town. The name was changed to Greensborough in 1791 after local land owners, and just after it had lost its bid to become the county seat of government to what is now Denton.

DENTON. Lady Caroline Calvert, for whom the county is named, married Sir Robert Eden, from 1769–76 last English colonial governor of Maryland. In 1773, when the county was established, Pig Point on the Choptank River was named its seat of government. Needing a more suitable name, it was renamed Eden–town, in honor of the governor. It quickly became shortened to Edenton. But Eden decided to cast his lot with the British and return to England at the start of the Revolution, so the E was dropped and the name became Denton. The Revolution caused postponement of the building of the courthouse, and Greensboro, farther up the Choptank River, vied to be the site until a referendum in 1790 resulted in Denton being selected.

Denton

There isn't much left in Denton from colonial times. On July 4, 1865, the Civil War had ended, and there was a major celebration underway, including brass band, a cannon fired every two minutes, firecrackers, Roman candles, and pin–wheels. Balls of candle–wick soaked in oil were batted back and forth until one lodged on a roof, and started a fire that wiped out the entire business district.

Sir Robert Eden is the ancester of Sir Anthony Eden, who followed Winston Churchill as prime minister of England.

TWO JOHNS. Down the Choptank Rivert about 5 miles from Denton are a point, housing development, and road named Two Johns. John Stewart Crossey and John Hart were vaudeville actors each of whom weighed over 300 pounds. They looked like twins and to capitalize on their appearance, used stage names of John Stewart Crossey and John Crossey Stewart. During the 1880s at the height of their careers they bought a farm here and called it The Two Johns, the name of their act. They expanded the farmhouse, built a wharf, and converted a warehouse into a dance pavillion and theatre. Friends arrived by steamboat, and parties were frequent. To keep the goodwill of suspicious neighbors, they once chartered a boat and invited the entire town of Denton to one of their shows. After a few years, they went broke and disappeared.

DOVER BRIDGE. Traveling east from Easton on MD 331, you cross the Choptank River to enter Caroline County. Dover is a lost town, a Choptank River port where a courthouse was planned in 1778 but was never built. Only the name of the bridge endures.

Bethlehem

BETHLEHEM. Once a year the post office is innundated with mail,- as collectors desire Christmas covers postmarked Bethlehem. The post office here stems from 1866, and the name may have been chosen by Methodist Bishop Francis Asbury.

HARMONY, 4 miles northeast of Bethlehem, implies "peace." Nearby, Charles Dickinson and Andrew Jackson met for the first time at a party. In 1806, the two men quarreled over a horse race and eventually fought a duel. Dickinson shot first and wounded Jackson. Jackson took careful aim and shot his opponent dead. Jackson was greatly criticized but that didn't help Dickinson, who is buried about a mile from Harmony.

PRESTON was originally called Snow Hill, when founded in 1845, but changed its name in 1856 because of the prominence of Snow Hill, seat of Worcester County. It is named after Alexander Preston, a prominent Baltimore lawyer of the time. Among its industries is the Preston trucking line, whose Preston 18–wheelers can be seen all over the U.S.

FEDERALSBURG. Marshyhope Creek, headwaters of the Northwest Fork of the Nanticoke River, splits the town, which was once called The Bridge because of a bridge here in 1792. Story has it that in 1812 a rousing meeting was held at The Bridge by the Federalist Party, complete with militia, drums and fifes, and stars and stripes. Patriotism was rampant, and to preserve the enthusiasm, the town was renamed Federalsburg. Republicans protested, politically they soon prevailed, and the Federalist Party declined in strength. Still the town's name remained. Unfortunately for the story, the name of the settlement appears in records as Federalsburgh as early as 1793, still likely named for the political party if not for the rousing meeting of 1812.

LINCHESTER is one of the oldest Caroline settlements, formerly called Murray's Mill for the grist mill that operated here as early as 1681. The mill that presently stands here probably was built in the mid–1800s. Linchester comes from a combination of CaroLINe and DorCHESTER counties, because the mill is on Hunting Creek which forms the border between the two counties.

MARYDEL, on the northern tip of the county, was called Halltown in 1850 for William Hall, who bought a tract of land here partly in Maryland and partly in Delaware. The name was changed to the combination of the two states in 1853.

In 1877 Marydel was scene of a duel – by then illegal – between James Gordon Bennett, owner and editor of the New York Herald, and Frederick May, a well–know explorer. One source says they quarreled over May's broken engagement to Bennett's sister, another says over Bennett's being accused of misbehavior in the May home while engaged to May's sister. Neither man was wounded, but Bennett exiled himself to Paris and ran the famous New York paper from there for the rest of his life.

HENDERSON was earlier called Meredith's Crossing, River Bridges, and Melville's Crossroads. In 1868, the Maryland and

Delaware Railroad reached the town, and its name was changed, for one of the railroad's directors.

GOLDSBORO was called Oldtown until the D & C Railroad reached it in 1867, at which time the townspeople wanted to give it a more modern name. Because the land around the village was owned by Dr. G. W. Goldsborough, the name was changed in 1870 to Goldsborough. There are also Goldsborough and Goldsborough Creek northwest of Easton in Talbot County. Goldsboroughs were prominent in colonial times in Maryland, originating with Nicholas Goldsborough of Dorset County, England, who arrived on Kent Island in 1670.

TALBOT COUNTY

TALBOT COUNTY was formed in 1661, then encompassing portions of Queen Anne's and Caroline counties. The present boundaries were established in 1706. The county is named for Grace Talbot, sister of Cecilius Calvert, second Lord Baltimore.

The 25 location names described in this chapter are arranged for north–south travelers on U.S. 50, which virtually splits the county down the middle and in a straight line. These names are followed by ones on the bayside of U.S. 50, and then ones on the inland side.

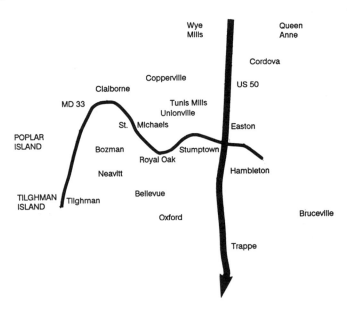

WYE RIVER forms part of the boundary between Queen Anne's and Talbot counties – indeed, the boundary runs right through the middle of Wye Mill. Some say the Wye was named because its course forms a "Y", others say it was named for the family of the Rev. William Wye who lived near it in the early 1700s. More likely it is named after the Wye River, which runs into the Severn, both in Wales. Evan Lloyd was a Welsh king who ruled lands between the Severn and Wye, and it was likely a Lloyd who named the river here.

The river gives its name to the village of **WYE MILLS**, just inside the northern border of the county, which contains Wye Mill (first in operation in 1672), and is adjacent to Wye Oak State Park, which preserves a massive white oak believed to be 400 years old, and Wye Church, which dates from 1721.

Also in the vicinity are Wye House, owned by the Lloyd family and at which Frederick Douglass spent his childhood; Wye Hall on Wye Island, summer home of William Paca, one of the four Maryland signers of the Declaration of Independence and governor of Maryland; and Wye Plantation, built in the 1600s and once owned by the Tilghmans.

Much of Talbot County early history concerns its aristocracy. Lloyds, Tilghmans, Goldsboroughs, and their kin – they frequently intermarried – were chosen for public office, while their ladies determined what and who were "acceptable." Perhaps the Lloyds were most powerful:

First Marylander Lloyd was Edward, probably born of an Edward Lloyd in Virginia, and by the 1640s leader of a Puritan group in Norfolk County. His name appears as one of several arrested in 1649 for refusing to attend the established Anglican church or hear the Book of Common Prayer. When these Puritans moved to Anne Arundal County, Maryland, Lloyd became the county's first chief executive and figured in the turbulent events of the 1650s, helping overthrow Lord Baltimore's regime in the name of Oliver Cromwell.

Lloyd moved to Talbot County about 1661, and built the first Wye House. He returned to England about 1668, and on his death in 1695 made his eldest grandson, Edward Lloyd II, his heir, and thus founded a dynasty that was one of the longest in America. Until this century a succession of men all named Edward Lloyd made Wye House their base as they won prominence in affairs of state. Edward was Speaker of the House, President of the Senate, and major general of the militia.

Henrietta Maria Lloyd, wife of Philemon Lloyd, was the wealthiest woman on the Eastern Shore, acknowledged social and business leader, strict, Catholic, and mother of twelve.

By 1770, Edward Lloyd III paid taxes on 12,390 acres of land in Talbot County, 12,467 in Dorchester, 5,859 in Queen Anne's, 5,216 in Kent, and 360 in Cecil. Edward IV acquired a town house and racing stable in Annapolis. Edward V possessed more than 500 slaves and was one of the nation's wealthiest wheat farmers. Edward VI extended the family estates to plantations in Mississippi, Arkansas, and Louisiana. Edward VII, who lived from 1825 to 1907, survived the disaster that the Confederate defeat meant to slaveholders and kept the Lloyd lands on a paying basis.

EASTON, seat of Talbot County, was at first the hamlet Pitts Bridge, which spanned an inlet of the Tred Avon River on the road north from Oxford. The first courthouse was built here in 1712, and the town was called Talbot Court House. By 1778, that was shortened to Talbot Town or Talbottown or just plain Talbot. By 1789, it had become the capital of the eastern shore and was called Easton, perhaps because of its location, more likely for Easton in Somersetshire, England, the county in which there's also the River Avon (see Tred Avon River).

The third Haven Quaker Meeting House, erected in 1682–84, and the courthouse of 1794 (enlarged in 1958) are among early structures that still stand.

STUMPTOWN is a settlement just south of Easton. There are at least three Stumptowns in Maryland, some perhaps named for Stump families, some for conspicuous stumps, none with definite origins.

HAMBLETON is 6 miles south of Easton, to the right of U.S. 50. To the left are the ruins of White Marsh Church. An important road of the 1700s led from the port of Oxford to White Marsh on to Dover – not Dover, Delaware, but the port along the Choptank at the east edge of the county (see Dover Bridge). Halfway between Oxford and Dover, about half mile west of the church, was a tavern and village called Hole–in–the–Wall, named perhaps because the tavern had a hole in its wall through which smuggled goods were passed in emergencies or named perhaps for its London counterpart.

In the late 1800s, post office authorities renamed the town. William Hambleton had been sheriff of Talbot County in 1663, and Samuel Hambleton, a descendent, for which the village was renamed, was a member of the House of Delegates, state senator, and in 1870, U.S. congressman.

TRAPPE is 8 miles south of Easton on U.S. 50. It seems certain that Trappe is not named after a Trappe family. What it is named after, however, is in doubt. There was a Trappist monastery, remains of which still exist. There was a flourishing colonial tavern called "The Partridge Trap," whose patrons talked about "visiting the Trap." And there were wolf traps in the area including a "Wolf trap bridge" mentioned in a deed of 1724. There are, however, Trappe villages or creeks in Wicomico, Somerset, and

Trappe

Worcester counties too, and likely all are named for the abounding animal traps.

Born just outside Trappe was John Dickinson, lawyer and colonial pamphleteer, later founder of Dickinson College at Carlisle, Pennsylvania. A conservative who hoped to reconcile with England, he opposed the Declaration of Independence. Still, he served as a General in the Revolution, drafted the Articles of Confederation, and as delegate from Delaware, advocated adoption of the Constitution in the 1787 National Convention.

COPPERVILLE, bayside of U.S. 50 in the northern portion of the county, is one of several towns – Unionville, Ivyville, Williamsburg, Hopkins Corner – that were built around churches or schools by former slaves, many of whom earned freedom by fighting for the Union in the Civil War. Copperville was founded by John Copper, who had been a slave at Wye Plantation.

TUNIS MILLS, just across Leeds Creek, apparently comes from John Hansel Tunis, who settled in Talbot County in the early 1800s. The mills were planing mills.

UNIONVILLE, a couple miles away, is one of at least four Maryland towns called Unionville or Uniontown and named in the patriotic wake of either the Revolutionary or Civil wars.

MILES RIVER, on which sits the town of St. Michaels, was spelled Miles River in 1782. The name was originally St. Michaels, commemorating St. Michael on whose feast day the colonists had to pay their semi–annual rents to the Calverts. It is thought that because of the Quakers who disliked titles, the "St." was removed from the name, and eventually the Marylander slurring of Michael made the name change further to Miles.

ST. MICHAELS, 8 miles west of Easton, retained its name whereas the river didn't. In 1667, Edward Elliott, an immigrant to Maryland, donated land for St. Michaels Church around which the village grew. St. Michaels became a major shipbuilding center, reaching its zenith in the 1820s.

Many Eastern Shore towns were terrified of attack by the British during the War of 1812, and St. Michaels was actually attacked on August 9, 1813. On August 6, the British landed about 2,000 troops on Kent Island, and rumors spread that St. Michaels was about to be attacked, because half a dozen vessels including one war ship were under construction here. Shortly after midnight on the rainy morning of August 10, 11 barges carrying about 300 British marines moored as close as possible to shore, and at 4 a.m. the troops disembarked. Most of St. Michaels' defenders immediately fled in panic, but a one–armed black man named John Stevens managed to turn one of the fort's guns on the attackers and fired at point–blank range a load that included a cannonball, chain shot, pieces of china, nails, lead bullets, and broken blass. Nineteen Britishers were killed by the blast, and the British retired and didn't land again. Stevens rushed to safety. It is said that more blood was shed by tavern arguments about who stayed and who ran than had been lost in the battle.

Another St. Michaels story is that the townspeople fooled the British by placing lanterns in the treetops so that enemy guns overshot the town. Another is that the only house hit was one on Mulberry Street where a cannonball crashed through the roof and thumped down the stairs into the main hall. The house still stands and is known as Cannonball House. But both of these stories apparently grew up later, as neither was recorded in the contemporary accounts of 1813.

CLAIBORNE, about 6 miles west of St. Michaels, was named for William Claiborne (see Kent Island). The village was established in 1866 as a ferry point between Baltimore and the Eastern Shore for what later (1890) became the Baltimore, Chesapeake, and Atlantic (BC&A) Railroad, which traversed the peninsula via St. Michaels, Easton, Salisbury, Berlin, to Ocean City. Travelers knew the BC&A as the Before Christ & After, or Black Cinders & Ashes.

During World War I, in which the military suffered 320,000 casualties, 548,000 Americans died from the worldwide flu epidemic. The BC&A issued to its employees a bottle of aspirin and quart of whiskey, with instructions to take four aspirin a day and a drink of whiskey at night as a preventative. Of course, some employees took four drinks of whiskey a day and an aspirin at night instead. It is reported that none got the flu.

Later, ferries also ran from Claiborne to Annapolis and Romancoke on Kent Island, one as late as the 1940s.

The stretch of land to the north of Claiborne is Rich Neck, home of the Tilghmans in the 1700s and 1800s, and where Matthew Tilghman is buried.

TILGHMAN ISLAND is the western tip of Talbot County, and includes the town of Tilghman and one called **FAIRBANKS** (named after Edward Ned Fairbanks, who was given the land for fighting in the War of 1812). Tilghman is a major name in Eastern Shore history, and there are many Tilghman decendents on the Eastern Shore today. Here are three Tilghman stories:

Tilghman Island was originally called the Great Choptank Island, because of its prominence in the mouth of the Choptank River. Col. Vincent Lowe arrived in America in 1672, married the daughter of Seth Foster, and acquired the island, then called Foster's Island, and changed the name to Lowes Island. Dr. Richard Tilghman came to America in 1657, and in 1670 was sheriff of Talbot County. His decendent, Matthew Tilghman, was a member of the Maryland legislature from 1751 until the Revolution, was called the "Patriarch of Maryland," and in 1783 "resorted to his estate at Tilghman's Point," by that time owning the island and changing its name for the final time.

That "Patriarch of Maryland" title was well deserved: Matthew was chairman of every delegation to the Continental Congress, Speaker of the House of Delegates, President of the convention in 1775 that established the Freemen of Maryland as the colony's de facto government, the person whose name headed the list of subscribers to the Articles of Association, and chairman or ranking member of every organizational body in Maryland from the Committee of Correspondence in 1774 to the Constitutional Convention that in 1776 wrote Maryland's first constitution.

More well known, if that's possible, was Tench Tilghman, Matthew's nephew and son–in–law, who was Maryland's Paul Revere. Lt. Col. Tilghman served as aide de camp to George Washington, and following the victory on October 19, 1781, at Yorktown, which ended the Revolutionary War, was the one selected to carry the official notice to the Continental Congress in Philadelphia. His trip is known as "Tilghman's Ride." It wasn't easy: He lost a night trying to cross from Virginia to Maryland when the skipper ran aground on the Tangier Island shoals, got becalmed off Annapolis, lost a full day crossing from Annapolis to Rock Hall because of mild breezes, and had to gallop the last hundred miles, arriving October 28.

Tench Tilghman, grandson of the above, served as major general of the Maryland militia just prior to the Civil War, but described his political position as "a little to the Southward of the South," and so was kept "on parole" at his home in Oxford by Union forces, having to pledge to say nothing during the War in opposition to the Union. His three sons, however, were among Tilghmans serving the Confederacy. In 1865, one, Tench Francis, helped Jefferson Davis flee southward from Richmond with the Confederate archives and the treasury, then about $25,000. Tilghman had charge of Davis' personal wagon, but on May 6 in Georgia, Davis rode ahead and was captured. His escorts decided to split up and return home. They buried the archives in a Florida barn, and split the treasury, Tench's share being $1,940.

POPLAR ISLAND, westernmost portion of Talbot County, about a mile off shore from Tilghman Island, was originally settled as early as 1632 by followers of William Claiborne (see Kent Island) and named for an associate, Lt. Richard Popeley. The island was named Popeleys, Popelese, Popleys, Poples, Poplies, Popplers, and Poplers, and eventually it was forgotten that there had ever been such a person, and the island was named Poplar under the impression it was named after trees that grew there.

One thing is certain about the Eastern Shore. Its boundaries are constantly changing. Poplar Island is now three islands: Poplar, Jefferson (on which there was a club visited by Presidents Roosevelt and Truman that burned in 1950), and Coaches, now all three belonging to the Smithsonian Institution, uninhabited, and shrinking.

SHARP'S ISLAND, 4 miles south of Tilghman's, is an even better example of the phenomenon. It was 700 acres in 1660, 438 acres in 1848, site of a resort hotel in the 1890s that was deserted by 1900, only 53 acres in 1918, and today nothing but a warning light in Choptank Bay.

BOZMAN is one of two towns on a neck of land between St. Michaels and Tilghman Island. It is named for settlers who arrived by 1663. John Leeds Bozman is credited with publishing the first history of Maryland in 1811.

NEAVITT is the second town, named after Henry Neavitt, who ran the general store when its post office was established.

ROYAL OAK is a town south of the Easton–St. Michaels road on MD 329 toward Bellevue. Story is that it was named for a famous large oak tree that was hit by two cannonballs fired by the British during the St. Michaels attack in 1813. However, the town seems to have been called Royal Oak before the War of 1812, albeit from the same giant oak.

Royal Oak

BELLEVUE – probably from beautiful view – is 4 miles further south, and is the site of the Bellevue–Oxford ferry. There's been a ferry here, across the Tred Avon River, since 1760, when Elizabeth Skinner started the line. The preseent ferry was built in 1923. It is the oldest ferry in the United States that runs free, un-attached to a cable.

OXFORD, 8 miles southeast of Easton, sits across from Bellevue on the Tred Avon River, and is named for the university town in England. It was settled as early as 1635, 30 acres were set aside for a town in 1668, and Charles Calvert proclaimed it a port of entry in 1669. It was officially laid out in 1683. It was a flourishing port until 1750.

Robert Morris, Sr., father of the Robert Morris who gained fame as "the financier of the Revolution," had his home in Oxford, in what is now the Robert Morris Inn. Indeed, the senior Morris dominated the economic life of the Bay community from the 1730s until 1750, at a time when Oxford was a prime port, with seven or eight ships reported in the harbor at once and many London trading firms with offices in the town.

In 1750, Morris had been aboard the *Liverpool Merchant*, which had just arrived, welcoming the captain. He climbed into a small boat to go ashore. The captain readied the ship's guns to fire a salute, as was custom, when a fly lit on his nose. His swat at the fly was misinterpreted by the crew, who fired the cannon prematurely, when Morris' boat was only 20 yards away. Wadding struck Morris' right arm, breaking it and inflicting a wound that became infected. Morris died six days later, only 39 years old and at the height of his career. He is buried at White Marsh Church (see Hambleton).

Only two men signed all three of the country's basic documents – the Declaration of Independence, Articles of Confederation, U.S. Constitution: Roger Sherman and Robert Morris, Jr.

TRED AVON RIVER, flows from Easton past Oxford, into the Choptank. Origin of the name is uncertain, it perhaps being derived from Third Haven, or a corruption of Thread Haven, or even Trade Haven. Or perhaps it stems from the River Avon in Somersetshire, England, which also has a town called Easton.

QUEEN ANNE, in the northeast corner of the county, just before one crosses into Caroline County, was a farm until railroad officials decided to put a station there in 1867, instead of at adjacent Hillsboro. The owner of the farm divided it into lots and simply watched the town begin to form. Although the village is virtually next door to Caroline County, it is part in Talbot and part in Queen Anne counties, taking its name from the latter.

CORDOVA is 8 miles northeast of Easton. A story says that once during railroad times – the village is on what was the Pennsylvania Railroad – a *CORD* of wood was left *OVER* here. A more likely source for the name is from Cordoba, Spain. Until the 1860s, a cross roads hamlet existed called Thimbletown. When the railroad arrived in 1869, the first stationmaster was told to find a more attractive name, and he leafed through a geography book until he found one he liked. Both of these stories are good – except that Cordova can be found on a map of 1866, three years before the railroad arrived.

BRUCEVILLE, 8 miles southeast of Easton, may take its name from the Bruce family. There is a Bruceville on land once owned by a Norman Bruce up in Carroll County.

DORCHESTER COUNTY

DORCHESTER COUNTY. The 27 names described in this chapter are arranged as their locations might be found while traveling U.S. 50 southward. A second group represent bayside locations, and a third group inland towns in the northern portion of the county.

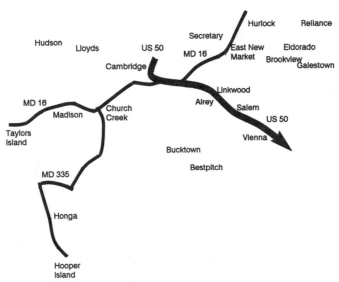

Exact date of establishment is unknown, but records indicate there was a county government in 1668. Dorchester is named for the Earl of Dorchester, a family friend of the Calverts.

CHOPTANK RIVER marks the boundary between Talbot and Dorchester counties. Choptank is from an Algonquian word meaning, essentially, "it flows back strongly," referring to tidal changes. The Choptank is the biggest Eastern Shore river, about 15 miles inland from Chesapeake Bay at Cambridge, and still 2 miles wide.

CAMBRIDGE. In 1683, the Maryland General Assembly passed the Act for the Advancement of Trade, which tried to legislate new towns into existence. Given the plantation economy of the time, purpose of the act was to provide places for the collection of royal customs and proprietary taxes on tobacco. The act says, "Noe merchant Factor or Mariner or other person whatsoever tradeing into this province" may trade at any except "Towns Ports and places here in this act before appointed," or face "forfeiting all such goods and merchandizes."

In 1684, in a supplement to the Act, a town was authorized in Dorchester County "Att Daniell Joansis plantation of the south side of the Greate Choptanke." That town was named in 1686 for the English university town. The county seat was moved to Cambridge, which may have contributed to its success as one of the very few legislated towns to ever materialize.

Cambridge became a major trading port, but lost its trade to Baltimore after the Revolution. Oystering became a major activity after the Civil War. Canning and fish–packing were big industries this century. By the 1960s, competition from California growers and those mass producing farm products caused the largest packers to close in Cambridge, putting nearly a third of the city and surrounding area out of work. On June 14, 1963, frustration spilled over into disorders in the city, precipitated by demonstrations against restaurants that refused to serve blacks. National attention was given the city when the governor sent in the National Guard, which stayed for a year. In 1964, Congress passed the Civil Rights Act, and tensions eased. Today there are prosperous factories and expanded port facilities, as the area witnesses an economic resurgence. The downtown area still follows the 1799 plat lines and provides a traveler with a totally different impression of the city than can be gathered from the main highway.

AIREY, 3 miles southeast of Cambridge, toward the major wildfowl refuges found in Dorchester County, has nothing to do with an aerie. Instead, it is named for Thomas Airey who arrived from Yorkshire, England, in 1726 and two years later became the priest of Great Choptank Parish. In 1781, the first Methodist sermon in the county was preached at the home of Henry Airey by Freeborn Garrettson, an itinerant preacher, who was promptly jailed for preaching doctrine of John Wesley, then considered a Tory. In the late 1800s the village moved north of its original location, to become a station on the Cambridge and Seaford Railroad.

Secretary

SECRETARY, about 5 miles upstream from Cambridge, was the name originally given to Secretary Creek, flowing into the Choptank River, and named for Henry Sewell, "Secretary of the Province of Maryland" in 1661 under Charles Calvert, then Governor. Sewell's home near the creek was considered "the government house of the Province."

"My Lady Sewell's Manor House" still stands at Secretary and is believed to have been built by Sewell in 1661. It had paneling, installed about 1720 or 1730 that was so fine it was given to, and can be seen at the Brooklyn Museum of Art. Lady Sewell? When Henry died in 1664, she married Charles, who later became third Lord Baltimore.

The town grew in the late 1800s and was incorporated in 1900, taking its name from the creek. But, the creek's name was changed to Warwick Creek, that name probably stemming from Sir Robert Rich, second Earl of Warwick (1587–1658) and head (in 1643) of a commission for the government of the colonies.

There had been a Warwick Fort Manor built in 1720 and over-looking Secretary Creek.

EAST NEW MARKET, a mile east of Secretary, was settled in 1660 on a major north–south Choptank Indian trail. A post for trading with the Indians was erected in 1767. Originally named Crossroads, the town became New Market, with a post office established by 1803. In 1927, the name was changed to East New Market, apparently to differentiate itself from New Market in Frederick County. There is also a Newmarket in St. Mary's County, and a couple of smaller New Markets in the state too. A popular name, the oldest Newmarket in the country is reported to be the one in New Hampshire, named in 1727, supposedly for Newmarket in County Suffolk, England.

HURLOCK, 4 miles from East New Market and about 13 miles northeast of Cambridge, developed around the Maryland and Delaware Railroad running east and west, and the Baltimore and Eastern Railroad running north and south. A railroad station was built in 1867, and John M. Hurlock erected the town's first store in 1869 and its first dwelling in 1872. The town was incorporated in 1892. It is said Hurlock won a tree–felling contest over another land owner in order to have the town named after him. The loser's name and what the town might have been called aren't recorded.

RELIANCE, at the northeastern border with Caroline County and Delaware, used to be called Johnson's Crossroads, for one Joe Johnson. He was the son–in–law and partner of a gang headed by notorious Lucretia "Patty" Cannon, a woman of charm, strength, and power. She masterminded the gang's operations, such as smuggling and kidnapping slaves and free Negroes for resale. Joe and Patty ran the tavern that stood at the Crossroads, often sending overnight guests to grissly deaths. The state line went right through the tavern, so that a combined raid by Maryland and Delaware police was needed to gain an arrest. One such raid was finally successful, and Patty and the gang were arrested, although Joe escaped. Patty was tried at Georgetown,

Delaware, confessed to at least 9 murders, and was sentenced to be hanged. While in jail, she committed suicide instead.

In 1882, the hamlet's name was understandably changed. Why it was changed to Reliance is unclear. The inn or a reconstruction of it dated 1885 (it's not clear which) still stands at the intersection of MD 577 and 392.

GALESTOWN, down southeast, on Gales Creek, may take its name from a Dr. Gale or Gales, no one seems sure. The village was apparently settled about 1833. There was a George Gale living in the county in 1790, but whether he was connected with the village is unclear.

MARSHYHOPE CREEK – river sized – flows down from Caroline County to join the Nanticoke. The "hope" part of the word is derived from Old English, and means region, in this case a region of marshes.

ELDORADO was originally called simply The Ferry, as early as 1671, for a ferry that ran between it and Brookview across Marshyhope Creek. The new name came from the name of a nearby farm.

BROOKVIEW. A ferry was established here in 1671, and the town was originally called Crochet's Ferry. The ferry crossed Marshyhope Creek to what is now Eldorado. A bridge was constructed over the creek in 1903, and the name changed to Brookview about the same time.

LINKWOOD, 6 miles southeast of Cambridge on U.S. 50, apparently was named because it did indeed connect two stands of woodland.

SALEM, 10 miles southeast of Cambridge, takes its name from the Bible, and means peace. A Methodist church was built in Salem in 1800, and the village became a Methodist settlement.

BUCKTOWN lies between U.S. 50 and the Blackwater Migratory Bird Refuge to the east. It isn't known whether this crossroads got its name from an abundance of deer or a family name. But just west of the crossroads is the birthplace of Harriet Tubman, who played a major role in the Underground Railroad, helping slaves escape to the north. She was illiterate and suffered from blackouts resulting from a head injury inflicted by a slave overseer, yet was considered highly dangerous by Maryland farmers, who offered large rewards for her capture. She herself escaped in 1849, but then made 20 trips back to Maryland to help others escape, especially from the Dorchester County area.

John Brown counted on her to lead an army of escaped slaves down from Canada to aid him in his raid upon Harper's Ferry. When the time came Harriet was sick and couldn't carry out the mission. During the Civil War she acted as a spy for the Union Army. Because she wasn't officially a soldier, Congress refused to recognize or compensate her for her services. She lived until 1913, mostly in Auburn, N.Y. In 1983, the United States finally honored her with a stamp in the Famous American series.

Bestpitch

BESTPITCH is an unmarked collection of a dozen or so houses next to the Transquaking River, east of U.S. 50, in the marshy swamp and forest that forms much of southern Dorchester County. There's no baseball field in the area. The name stems from a farmer named Bestpitch in the area in the late 1600s.

TRANSQUAKING RIVER, which flows from the Linkwood area through the marshes of central Dorchester County, is attributed to an Algonquian word meaning "place of the white cedar swamp." Algonquian, by the way, refers to the group of Indian languages spoken, but not written, from Labrador to the Carolinas to the Great Plains.

VIENNA, on the Nanticoke River, is first mentioned in a law of 1706, which ordered the area to be laid out as one of sites established "for the advancement of trade." The site bordered the reservation set aside for the Nanticoke Indians in 1698. The site had been formerly called Emperors Landing, and the name of Vienna is believed to be derived from the name of the Nanticoke Emperor Vinnacokasimmon or Unnacocassinon. A State Road Commission sign at Vienna reads: Unnakokossimmon Emperor to the Nanticoke Indians Lived (about 1677) at Chicacone, an ancient Indian town north of this point.

About 1768, Vienna became a port of entry with its own customs official, and the customs house, in use from 1791 to 1866, still stands today, although in disrepair. By 1781, its shipyards were considered worthy of attack by the British. A brig was burned in the shipyard, and the British killed Levin Dorsey, only man to die on Dorchester soil during the Revolution.

Biggest building in Vienna today, just south of the new highway bridge and on the Nanticoke, is the electric generating plant of the Delmarva Power and Light Company. The plant was built in 1928 and does not generate power from the river, but from oil, brought up the river by tankers. There was a bridge across the Nanticoke at Vienna in 1828, but it was removed because it was a menace to navigation, and replaced with a ferry. A highway bridge was again built in 1931, and served until the current one was opened in 1989.

NANTICOKE RIVER forms the boundary between Dorchester and Wicomico counties. The word designates the river, a village on the river, and the group of early Maryland Indians. It comes from the Algonquian meaning "tidewater people – they who ply the tidewater stream."

LLOYDS, 6 miles west of Cambridge as one travels toward the Bay, stems from the Lloyd family name, perhaps more associated with Wye House in Talbot County than this location.

HUDSON, in the northwest corner of the county, reflects an old Eastern Shore family name, stemming from at least the 1700s, and sometimes written Hudson, Hodson, or Huttson. There are also Hudsons Corner in Somerset and a Hudson's Corners up in Cecil counties.

CHURCH CREEK, a village 6 miles southwest of Cambridge, on Church Creek, which flows into the Little Choptank River, is known for the Treaty Oak, under which one of the first conferences with the Indians took place about 1650, and Old Trinity Church, the oldest Episcopal Church still standing in Maryland. The church was built about 1675, and was restored in 1850 and again in 1956. The church still has a communion chalice presented by Queen Anne, and the altar is believed to be the original. In the adjacent graveyard lie Thomas King Carroll, governor of Maryland in 1830, and his daughter, Anna Ella Carroll (see Kingston). There are Church Creek names in at least five other Maryland counties.

MADISON, about 10 miles from Cambridge, is likely named for James Madison, who became president in 1809, although there was a village here as early as 1760, and as recently as 1866 it was called Tobacco Stick. That name came from an Indian who escaped pursuers by vaulting across a creek on a tobacco stick. Emerson Harrington, Maryland governor during World War I, was born here.

TAYLOR'S ISLAND, westernmost portion of the county, was named for Thomas Taylor, an early settler. The island was inhabited a decade before the county was laid out.

HOOPER ISLAND, southwesternmost portion of the county, is actually Upper, Middle, and Lower Hooper islands, with Hoopersville the terminus of the road on Middle Hooper Island.

The islands were settled by Catholics from St. Mary's County, including Hoopers, Tubmans, Meekins, and others, with the name accredited to Henry Hooper, "a gentleman's justice," who arrived in 1667 and owned the land on the upper island.

HONGA RIVER, flowing toward the Bay, between the Hooper Islands and the mainland, has early spellings of Hunger, Hungar, even Hungary. Honga appears to be an abbreviation of Indian "kahunge," or goose.

BLOODSWORTH ISLAND, the southwestern–most portion of Dorchester County, and one of the largest islands in the Chesapeake, was named for the Bloodwworth family. It is now low and swampy – and government owned.

WICOMICO COUNTY

WICOMICO COUNTY was settled in the early 1700s, and the City of Salisbury was laid out in 1732. Wicomico didn't become a county until 1867, when it was "cut out" of Somerset and Worcester counties. The name is a combination of Indian words, perhaps "wicko" meaning house, not unlike wigwam, which means lodge, with a connotation of round. The "melee" portion means building, as in "there are buildings," apparently connoting an Indian town on the river.

The 15 locations in this chapter are arranged as one travels eastward on U.S. 50, except for an excursion back toward Chesapeake Bay starting with MD 349.

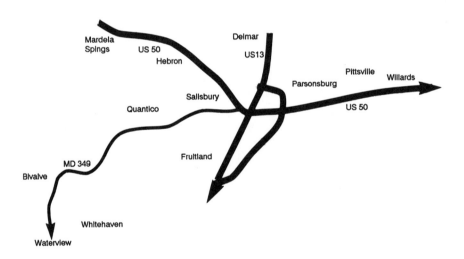

MARDELA SPRINGS does have a natural sulpher spring, a stopping place on an Indian trail before white settlers and site of a hotel and health resort in the late 1800s. The town was originally called Barren Creek, located on the creek of the same name, probably derived from a family name Baron or Barren. The name was changed in 1906 to the combination of MARyland and DELAware, the corner of which is only a couple miles away.

HEBRON, a mile west of U.S. 50, was most likely named for the bibilical town in the 1890s when it grew around the railroad.

QUANTICO, 5 miles further west, derives from Algonquian, but there is disagreement over its meaning. One source says essentially "the dancing place," another says "at the long creek," Quantico being on Quantico Creek, which is about eight miles long. The town dates from the 1700s.

WHITEHAVEN, 10 miles or so southwest of Quantico, on the Wicomico River, was established about 1700 by Col. George Gale, an Anglican who arrived from Whitehaven in Cumberlandshire, England. It hasn't been established whether this is the same Gale who was connected with Galestown.

BIVALVE is further toward Chesapeake Bay, on the Nanticoke, on the county's northwest border. It was originally Waltersville, for a local resident, but was changed in 1887 when a post office was established, at the suggestion of its postmaster. A bivalve is an animal with two shells, like a clam, in this case an oyster, oystering and oyster packing being main occupations of the village, along with water sports, fishing, and to a lessening degree, muskrat trapping.

WATERVIEW is at the western end of the county, within view of where the Nanticoke and Wicomico rivers meet to flow into Tangier Sound and then Chesapeake Bay. Twenty years ago the quiet village made the news when the Russian Embassy in Washington suddenly rented an old hotel here for the summer.

Rockawalkin

ROCKAWALKIN Road, Ridge, Creek, and once village, back close to U.S. 50 south of Hebron, all bear the peculiar name. A settler named Rock refused to ride a horse, and his neighbors would say "Here comes Rock a–walkin'." Or, Indian derivations can yield "place of the fork in the stream" or "at the sandy ground." Or, the Wicomico River was originally called Rockiawackin, and 1697 records mention the "Nations of the Rockawakinmany." Too, the utterance of a town drunk and the name of a sacred Indian stone have been mentioned as sources. Take your pick.

SALISBURY was settled by landowners from the vicinity of Salisbury, Wiltshire, England. One of the first, John Rhodeson, acquired 200 acres in the area in 1667 and gave the Salisbury name to his land. In 1732, the General Assembly authorized Salisbury Town at what had been called Handy's Landing on the Wicomico River.

For many years, Salisbury lay in both Somerset and Worcester counties, with appropriately–named Division Street as the boundary. When Wicomico County was formed in 1867, Salisbury become its seat of government.

Fires in 1860 and 1886 destroyed early structures, so that only one pre–Victorian house, Poplar Hill Mansion, built in 1795 for Major Handy, remains.

Originally the river was a main travel route, but later both railroad and motor routes converged on Salisbury. As motor traffic increased, Salisbury grew, now being the major commercial center for the lower Eastern Shore.

Any traveler who stops on U.S. 50 at a red light near the river and next to a Perdue processing plant (one of six) can attest that a major industry is poultry and poultry products. Delmarva peninsula numbers are staggering: 300,000 eggs are put into incubation each day. It takes roughly 18 days to hatch and 7 weeks to grow broilers averaging 4–1/2 pounds. About 500 million such broilers are produced annually. Perdue, Holly Farms, Con Agra (Country Pride), Showell Farms (Cookin' Good), and Cargill are among major producers with Delmarva operations.

Fruitland

FRUITLAND, just south and virtually a suburb of Salisbury, in the 1840s was called Forkland, perhaps because of a fork in the road. The town grew into a canning and shipping center when the railroad arrived in 1867. By 1873 when the railroad was more important than the old road, residents voted to choose between newly suggested names of Phoenix or Fruitland. The original big–crop fruit of the area was strawberries.

DELMAR, about 5 miles directly north of Salisbury, began as a town in 1859, after the Delaware Railroad reached the DELaware–MARyland line in 1858 and established repair shops here. The main street is the state line, with businesses and residences on both sides, and the town operates with two mayors, two town councils, two school systems, and outlooks toward two states, but with one post office and the single combined name.

PARSONBURG, 7 miles east of Salisbury, wasn't originally a preacher's town. It was named after the Parsons, local farmers, millers, and carpenters in the mid–1800s.

PITTSVILLE, 3 miles further east, was named after the president of the Wicomico and Pocomoke Railroad, which was completed in 1868 from Salisbury to Berlin as a continuation of the line from Claiborne. The man in question is listed in one source as William Pitts, in another as Dr. H. R. Pitts.

WILLARDS, another 3 miles further east, began as a station named for Willard or Willards Thompson of Baltimore, an executive of the railroad that crossed the town.

POCOMOKE RIVER forms the boundary between Wicomico and Worcester counties. Its headwaters are in the Great Pocomoke Swamp, about 50 square miles along the Delaware and Maryland border, where pine, gum, holly, cedar, and cypress can be found. The swamp was so dense, maps almost as late as 1900 showed little detail of the area.

From colonial times, cypress shingles from this area were used in houses throughout the region for roofs and siding. By the 1860s, original timber was gone, but layers of fallen cypress and cedar were found in the peat of the swamp and excavated during rainy seasons. The Great Fire of 1930, which raged for months during a drought, burned off 5 to 10 feet of the peat, including most of the remaining cypress and cedar.

But the swamp and many of its trees sill exist, and the headwaters of the Pocomoke remain hard to access, its waters dark because of tangled growth close to its shores, and in its own way, it remains mysterious. The name Pocomoke comes from the Algonquian, and depending on how it is translated, means something like "it pierces or breaks the ground."

SOMERSET COUNTY

SOMERSET COUNTY forms the southern–most county on the Eastern Shore, separated from Wicomico County on the north by the Wicomico River, from Virginia on the south by the Pocomoke River, and from Worcester County on the east by the Pocomoke and its tributary, Dividing Creek.

In 1659–60, Virginia framed a law against Quakers: "an unreasonable and turbulent sort of people who daily gather together unlawful assemblies of people, teaching lies, miracles, false visions, prophecies, and doctrines tending to disturb the peace, disorganize society and destroy all law and government and religion." The act called for no more entry of Quakers and removal of those living in Virginia. The Quakers could take a hint when they saw one, and began plans to move, many to the isolated, unsettled southern portion of the Maryland eastern shore. By 1661 they had petitioned and received approval from Cecilius Calvert, second Lord Baltimore, through Governor Philip Calvert, to become the first settlers there. In 1666, Somerset was proclaimed a

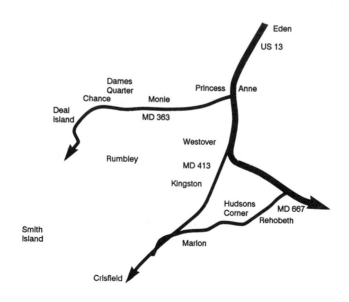

43

county – encompassing what are now portions of Wicomico and Worcester counties – and named for Mary Somerset, sister–in–law of Cecilius.

Three necks of land toward the Bay are formed by the Wicomico, Manokin, Annemessex, and Pocomoke Rivers, and the 17 locations described in this chapter are arranged as one travels north to south through the county, and westward along those necks.

EDEN, just inside the border on U.S. 13, was named for Governor Robert Eden (see Denton).

PRINCESS ANNE is about six miles south of Eden. Queen Anne (see Queen Anne's County) had 17 children, 12 of whom died a short time after birth and the others quite young. Upon her death in 1714, succession passed from the Stuarts to the Hanoverians, George I ruling 1714–27 and George II 1727–60. George II had three sons and five daughters, one of whom was a princess named Anne and who married, in 1734, Prince William of Orange.

For early settlers, the head of navigation on a river was almost always site of a town, transfer point from boats to land transportation. The village at the head of Manokin River was Princess Anne, laid out in 1733. It was named for the princess. Its main street was named Prince William Street for her husband. It became the county seat in 1742 when Worcester County was split off and the old courthouse at Dividing Creek was too far away from the center of the new county area.

Princess Anne still retains its colonial atmosphere, with several early buildings, one a private cottage built in 1705, another the Washington Hotel built in 1744, still in use.

MANOKIN RIVER was called Monacans when Captain John Smith first saw it in 1608. It likely stems from an Algonquian name meaning approximately "where the earth is dug out."

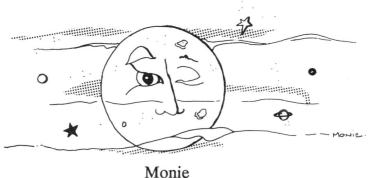

Monie

MONIE is a half–dozen miles west of Princess Anne toward the Bay. Monie is a hamlet, and there are two Monie creeks and a Monie bay nearby. Monie is said somewhat like Moon–EYE, and its derivation isn't clear. It could be from similar words in Algonquian that mean island or deep, except it has been pointed out that none of these waters are deep and Monie isn't an island.

DAMES QUARTER is a town, about 10 miles west of Princess Anne, amidst the Dames Quarter Marsh and Deal Wildlife Management Area. It was formerly (1670) known as Damnd (sic) Quarter, perhaps because of its proximity to Deal Island.

DEAL ISLAND, about 14 miles west of Princess Anne on Chesapeake Bay, was originally called Devil's Island. There were many Scots in the area, and their word for Devil was Deil, so the island was spelled Deil's Island and evolved into Deal Island. Another story says that an elder of one of the Methodist churches had the names of both Devil's Island and Damned Quarter changed, so no one would think Satan had any right or property here.

CHANCE is just north of Deal. Story goes that a Capt. James Whitelock proposed Rock Creek as the name for the place, but postal authorities disapproved. He then proposed Chance, because chances were there wouldn't be a post office at all. Success was achieved, and the post office was named Chance.

WESTOVER, about six miles south of Princess Anne, off U.S. 13 toward Crisfield, is a truck and rail center for the surrounding farm community. There was a Westover Farm in colonial days, and more recently a Westover Manor nearby, but it is believed the name is not from a local family name, but instead comes from Westover in Somersetshire, England.

RUMBLEY is about 10 miles west of Westover, on the Bay, near **FRENCHTOWN**, on the neck formed by the Manokin and the Big Annemessex Rivers. Researchers have tried to determine whether Rumbley derives from something rumbling, or from an early Rumbly family. Frenchtown might have come from French Acadian refugees in 1755, or from a family name, French. In both cases, the origins seem unclear.

ANNEMESSEX RIVER comes from the Algonquian for "It flies beneath [the bank]." There are two: the Big Annemessex to the north and the Little Annemessex at Crisfield.

KINGSTON, about 4 miles southwest of Westover on MD 413 toward Crisfield, takes its name from the King family. Nearby Kingston Hall was built in the late 1700s by Thomas King, whose forebears included Robert King of Ireland, first of his name to settle in Maryland and whose grandson, Thomas King Carroll, became governor of Maryland in 1830.

Governor King's first daughter, Anna Ella Carroll, grew up at Kingston Hall to become famous as an unacknowledged member of Lincoln's cabinet. After her father's death, she became an abolitionist. She is credited with saving Maryland for the Union by publishing a pamphlet in answer to a speech by Sen. Breckinridge of Kentucky and distributing 50,000 copies at her own expense. President Lincoln noted the favorable effect the pamphlet had, and encouraged her to continue writing. Later, he sent her to St. Louis to write of the proposed Union expedition down the Mississippi toward Vicksburg. She wrote that the river was too heavily fortified for the expedition to succeed and recommended that attack should be through the Tennessee Valley. Her strategy was accepted. When the capture of Vicksburg seemed impossible, Miss Carroll drew plans for attack from the land, and in 1863, Vicksburg did fall from land attack. Union generals were never told that such strategies had been developed by a woman, and when Lincoln died, she never received the credit due her, Congress didn't reward her, and she was forgotten. She lived in Washington until 1894, supported by her sister.

MARION, 4 miles further toward Crisfield, was a town many years before it had a name. When the railroad arrived, John Horsey donated land for the railroad, and the town was named for his daughter. The Horsey name goes back to Stephen Horsey, first known settler in Maryland below the Choptank in 1663.

CRISFIELD, 13 miles west of U.S. 13, is on the Bay – actually on the waters of Tangier Sound and the Little Annemessex River. It was platted in 1663, first known as Annemessex, then Somers Cove, the latter after Benjamin Somer or Summer; the large marina in town is still called Somers Cove marina.

The present name comes from John Crisfield who financed the Eastern Shore Railroad in Maryland. That railroad ended at Delmar (see Delmar), and he was able to bring it through Salisbury, Princess Anne, and down to Crisfield, opening up markets for southwestern Eastern Shore products from strawberries to crabs. There are over a dozen seafood processing plants still at work in Crisfield, although in its heyday about 1860 there were 190. His task wasn't easy, because of the marshland. But that problem was solved: The railroad bed – indeed portions of Crisfield itself – are built atop tons of oyster shells.

SMITH ISLAND, about 6 miles into the Bay from Crisfield, is Maryland's southern most point in the Bay. Tangier Island, further south, is in Virginia. Smith Island is appropriately named for John Smith, who discovered it in 1608.

HUDSONS CORNER, about 5 miles east of Marion enroute back toward U.S. 13 on MD 667 toward Pocomoke City, takes its name from the Hudson family. See Hudson.

REHOBETH is a village on the Pocomoke River halfway between Hudsons Corner and Pocomoke City. The Biblical name means "there is room," and it was given to his Pocomoke River plantation by Col. William Stevens when he patented it in 1665. Stevens became a county justice that same year, and served as a member of the council until from 1679–87, amassing a fortune from real estate and business. Rehobeth became a place of trade and commerce.

It also became the cradle of organized Presbyterianism in America. In 1683, Rev. Francis MaKemie arrived from Ireland in answer to a request by Col. Stevens that someone be sent to minister the spiritual needs of Presbyterians in the area. Rev. Makemie not only did so, but extended his travels from Europe to Barbados – even to Philadelphia from which organized Presbyterianism in America grew. Rehobeth contained both its parish church (Church of England) and the Meeting House of the Rehobeth Congregation of the Presbyterian Church, first such building in America, ruins of which still stand today. Rehobeth can claim the foundation, if not the origin, of the Presbyterian Church in America.

WORCESTER COUNTY

WORCESTER COUNTY, named for the Earl of Worcester, was originally part of Somerset County, but was established separately in 1742. Worcester is Maryland's only land on the Atlantic seacoast.

The 22 communities and names described in this chapter include Whaleysville and Berlin alongside U.S. 50 as it continues to Ocean City, and then 14 alongside U.S. 113 from north to south.

WHALEYSVILLE. There's disagreement whether it's named after Edward, Seth, or Peter. Or whether it was originally really Whaley, Walley, Whale, or Wale.

One legend persists that General Edward Whaley, who in 1649 was instrumental in the execution of Charles I (like casting the deciding vote to have him beheaded), hid out in this area, and that many other Whaley family members are his descendents. Believed founded before 1672, Whaleysville was thought to be an intentionally hidden village, hidden in the huge cypress

49

swamp that existed along what is now the Maryland–Delaware border. Published maps show the area as uninhabited until after 1805.

One account found an Edware Wale in the Pocomoke area in 1666. He moved to the Sinepuxent region in 1676. Was that General Edward Whaley?

Other tales say the locality was first called Mitchell's Store, then about 1720, Turn in the Road. It wasn't named Whaleysville until 1850, then for Capt. Peter Whaley. Other sources claim it was named for Captain Seth Whaley, settler in the 1700s.

Near Whaleysville today on MD 346 less than a mile from U.S. 50 is an evergreen grove, behind which is the Whaley Cemetery, with a brick wall and very neat grounds. One of its oldest graves: Captain Peter Whaley, 1779–1860. And on a nearby corner, near a turn in the road, stands Mitchell's store, dated 1666.

BERLIN, halfway between the Worcester County line and Ocean City, was built on land patented and named Burleigh Plantation by Col. William Stevens, who also founded Rehobeth and Pocomoke City, in 1677. The present name comes from a slurring of Burleigh or Burley Inn that stood here, and is pronounced with accent on the first syllable and not on the last like the German capital.

Born in Berlin in 1779 was Stephen Decatur. His mother had come to the area from Philadelphia to escape the British occupation and protect her pregnancy. Within a year, she returned to Philadelphia. Stephen grew to become a major naval hero, with successes against the pirates of the Barbary Coast and against the British during the War of 1812.

ASSAWOMAN BAY. There's a series of oceanside bays, islands, and sounds with intriguing Indian names in the county. Northernmost is Assawoman Bay, which MD 90, expressway to upper Ocean City, crosses. "Assa" comes from Algonquian and means either "across," which is usually accepted, or "yellow." Since the Indians didn't leave their languages in written form, many of their words have remained untranslated, and "woman" is one, so the meaning of the entire word remains unsolved. **ISLE OF WIGHT BAY** lies just to the south, named for its counterpart in the English Channel. South of Ocean City is **ASSATEAGUE**, site of state park and national seashore. "Teague" comes from an Indian word meaning "flow" and implying a stream or river, so that Assateague means either "river across" or "yellow river." Largest bay is southernmost **CHINCOTEAGUE**, with "chinco" being derived from the Indian for "large," and the word appropriately meaning "large river."

OCEAN CITY, eastern terminus of U.S. 50, was initially patented by William Wittington in 1711, and for over a century, the main use of the barrier island that was to become Ocean City was that of grazing animals. The land wasn't very good, and animals could be pastured only during plant–growing season.

The first structure was the Rhode Island Inn, built, owned, and managed by Issac (sic) Coffin, in 1869.

In the early 1870s, a group of investors calling themselves the Sinepuxent Beach Corporation secured 10 acres from the New York financier who owned the land, journeyed by stage and carriage, crossed Assawoman Bay in boats, and physically mapped out the first resort – complete with the names that stand today – Baltimore and Philadelphia avenues and the streets named for the Maryland counties.

It was in the mid–1800s that people first began vacationing seaside to escape the heat and air of crowded cities. Until then, most men couldn't swim and women avoided water altogether. The name therefore had to be attractive to interest women at all. So the first resort was actually named as "The Ladies Resort to the Ocean."

Ocean City

The name, Ocean City, came into use right away, in the early 1870s.

By 1874 the Wicomoco & Pocomoke Railroad added an extension from Berlin to the bay, and by 1876 added a trestle taking the line into downtown Ocean City.

The boardwalk was added in the 1880s, and by 1897 ran all the way to 8th Street.

By the 1930s, the town had grown to 15th Street. Some local people wanted to establish an inlet, linking Assawoman Bay with the Atlantic. On August 23, 1933, Mother Nature settled that issue, via the city's most vicious hurricane, whose wake and surge tides created the inlet, leveled the fishing camps south of the inlet, and destroyed the railroad entrance to the city.

In 1951, Harrison Hall at 15th Street became the northermost hotel in the city. In 1962, a hurricane cut another inlet across the barrier at 70th Street, but receding waters re–established the land there. And it may be hard to believe, but all of the city's high–rise development has occurred only since 1965.

BISHOPVILLE and **BISHOP** lie near U.S. 113 just inside the Delaware line. Henry Bishop arrived in Maryland in 1634 in the original group that founded St. Marys City. By 1643 he had apparently moved to the Eastern Shore, and in 1666 acquired a patent for 2,300 seaside acres from Virginia; two years later when the Virginia–Maryland line was agreed upon, the acreage was found to be in Maryland. He acquired further lands, some in Delaware. A mill was created in the Bishopville area in the 1700s, and was eventually purchased by decendent Littleton Bishop in 1836. By 1878, Bishopville was prosperous community of 350, thriving on timber yields.

SHOWELL is a mile to the south. Samuel Showell was in the St. Martins area in 1689, and his descendents were farmers, timbermen, storekeepers, and tavern managers. In the late 1800s, Lemuel Showell III (called Col. although no one now knows why) made two major contributions: He struggled for years to bring a railroad to the county and to create a seaside resort. He succeeded in both, becoming president of the Wicomico and Pocomoke Railroad, and building the first cottage on the beach in Ocean City. The town that had been called St. Martins was changed during his lifetime to Showell to show the appreciation of area residents.

An additional noteworthy native of the Bishop and Showell area was Dr. George Bunting, who developed Noxema.

OCEAN PINES started in 1968 when U.S. Land, Inc., acquired nearly all of Jenkins and Turville Necks and planned about 10,000 lots. Ocean Pines today encompasses over 8,000 residences and a tax base larger than the other towns of Worcester County combined (except for Ocean City) – but is still unincorporated. The name derives from original large stands of pine, more pines added along its main roads, and its location on the St. Martin's River and Isle of Wight Bay opposite Ocean City.

TAYLORSVILLE, south of Showell on MD 589, is at the head of Turville Creek, site of Laban J. Taylor's Mill in the mid–1800s. The mill apparently served as both sawmill and grist mill. MD 589 passes over the old spillway.

IRONSHIRE, south of Berlin, stems not from iron, but from a family name, perhaps Ironshier.

NEWARK is about halfway between Berlin and Snow Hill. There are so many Newarks that the railroad changed the name of the station here to Queponco Station. Newark has nothing to do with "ark," but instead comes from the old English, meaning "new work." Queponco is Indian, with the nicest possible meaning being "limit of the sands." Other translations seem to be "pine tree dust" or "full of sand flies."

BASKET SWITCH, a mile south, did indeed have a basket factory next to the switch on the old Pennsylvania Railroad.

Snow Hill

SNOW HILL, unlike Basket Switch, had neither snow nor hill. The area was patented by Col. William Stevens in 1676 and was likely named for the Snow Hill section of London by him or by early settlers who came from there. Col. Stevens sold his land to Henry Bishop in 1685, an act was passed establishing a town or port at Snow Hill in 1686, and the town was officially created in 1688. Snow Hill grew as the most important town in the county, and became seat of government when the county was created in 1742.

NASSAWANGO FURNACE, 4 miles west of Snow Hill, was built in 1832 to process bog ore from the creek. Only high prices for iron could justify making it from such low–grade material, and by 1847, the furnace was abandoned. During the two decades, a village of over 200 grew up, but today ruins only of the furnace itself remain. Nassawango translates from the Indian to something like "between the streams."

BOXIRON, 6 miles southeast of Snow Hill, gets its name from bog's iron, and there were once factories here making pig iron from the bog iron oxide.

GIRDLETREE, about 7 miles southeast of Snow Hill, has several stories connected with its name: An Indian girdled a tree for garden space. A wild grapevine girdled a tree at this spot. Surveyors girdled or marked a tree here. Charles Bishop is said to have settled here prior to the Civil War and removed a big beech tree by girdling it before building his home; he called his farm Girdle Tree Hill. Girdling a plant or tree means cutting around it, to cut off the nutrients and kill it, as opposed to cutting it all the way through and felling it.

STOCKTON, about 5 miles east of Klej Grange, was formerly Sandy Hill, but became Stock Town in pre–rail days when it was a southern assembly point for cattle to be herded overland to Wilmington for slaughter. When the railroad came near, the name was changed to Hursley, because of too many Stocktons, but when the railroad connection collapsed, the name reverted.

KLEJ GRANGE lies halfway between Snow Hill and Pocomoke City. The hamlet was known as Scratch Gravel, Turkey Trap, Traptown, and Lindseyville. In the 1870s, plans called for a railroad to arrive, and Joseph Drexel, the Philadelphia–New York financier, purchased several thousand acres and planned to industrialize the hamlet and intensify land cultivation. None of the hamlet names, however, suited his efforts, and Klej Grange was chosen instead. Klej represented the first letters of Mr. Drexel's daughters' names: Katherine, Louise, Elizabeth, and Jane. Grange suggested granary or abundance. Mr. Drexel died in 1888, development did not occur, and Klej Grange remains a hamlet, but the name endures.

POCOMOKE CITY, where U.S. 113 and 13 join, takes its name from the river (see Pocomoke River). It had several prior names, which have been listed as: Steven's Ferry in 1670, Meeting House Landing (1683), Warehouse Landing (1700), Newton or New Town (1780), and Pocomoke City (1878).

Col. William Stevens had been in Cromwell's army and come to America after Cromwell's death. His ship was wrecked at Assateague, and Indians guided him to Accomack. In 1660, he left Virginia for Maryland. He was Somerset's first representative in the general assembly, a deputy governor of Maryland, and member of Lord Baltimore's council. He was also the original ferryman–keeper at what is now Pocomoke City and is considered the originator of the city.

WHO WERE THOSE LORDS BALTIMORE, ANYWAY?

GEORGE CALVERT, 1ST LORD BALTIMORE – George was born in Yorkshire, England, about 1580, son of a gentleman. He obtained his BA from Trinity College, Oxford, in 1597, and toured Europe, studying French, Italian, and Spanish. In 1604, he married Anne Mynne.

In 1606, George began his public career as a secretary to Robert Cecil, secretary of state, who needed foreign language specialists on his staff. When Cecil died in 1612, George continued to aid James I, eventually handling all Spanish and Italian correspondence. He was knighted in 1617, and named secretary of state himself in 1619. By 1625, Puritanism was forcing Catholics like George from state positions, and he resigned. James I rewarded him with a barony in the Irish peerage, because he held lands in Ireland as well as in Yorkshire. George assumed the title Lord Baltimore.

George had been interested in the American colonization for some time, serving in the Virginia Company among others. In 1621, he established a colony in Newfoundland, but after one winter, sought a warmer clime. In 1629, he went to Virginia, and by 1632, the crown, then Charles I, granted unsettled territory northeast of the Potomac to its friend.

George wanted the colony named Avalon, same as he had used in Newfoundland. Charles thought it would be nice, however, if it were named after his wife, Henrietta Maria, and so it became Maryland.

George modeled his charter on that of the medieval palatinate of Durham, which gave founders supreme power. But he also included statements that bade toleration of all Christian religions, a remarkable move for the time.

George died in April 1632 before the charter was sealed. The charter was issued to his son Cecil in June.

CECILIUS CALVERT, 2ND LORD BALTIMORE – Cecilius or Cecil followed his father's path through Trinity College. In 1628 he married Anne Arundell. He inherited his father's charter when he was 26, and for the next 43 years, served as proprietor of Maryland, but because of personal and political enemies fighting over state and religious differences was never able to leave England to see his lands. He delegated the running of the colony to his younger brother, Leonard, whom he sent to Maryland with some colonists in 1633, and later, his son Charles. His accomplishments included guaranteeing during religious turbulent times religious liberty to all who accepted the doctrine of the Trinity, and trying to make good his claims to all territory within his grant. Cecil died in 1675.

LEONARD CALVERT – Leonard was first governor of Maryland, and it was he who arrived with about 220 settlers in 1634, making their first settlement at St. Marys, and landing on Kent Island.

In defending the colony's boundaries, Leonard fought for years William Claiborne, the Virginian who had permission to trade on Kent Island and tried to establish permanent rights to the territory. These fights were complicated by the civil war in 1642 that saw the Commonwealth created in England under Oliver Cromwell, Leonard's trip to England to discuss such matters with Cecil, and while he was gone an armed invasion of St. Marys by Richard Ingle allied with Claiborne. Although they seized control of Maryland, Leonard returned and re–established control by 1646. He died in Maryland in 1647, having served as governor, but as Cecil was still alive, never having obtained the proprietorship or gaining the title Lord Baltimore.

CHARLES CALVERT, 3RD LORD BALTIMORE – Charles was born 1637, son of Cecil, who sent him to Maryland as governor when he was 24. Upon Cecil's death in 1675, Charles succeeded to the title and went to England the next year to settle matters like navigation rights on the Potomac and defense against the Indians. From 1679 to 1684 he was back governing the colony, but then returned to England to defend his property rights against William Penn. In 1689 a Protestant rebellion led by John Codde overthrew his government in Maryland, and in 1691 the crown withdrew his authority to govern, although he retained the property rights. He never returned to Maryland, and died in February 1715.

BENEDICT LEONARD CALVERT, 4th LORD BALTIMORE – The son of Charles, Benedict was the first Lord Baltimore to embrace the Anglican faith, presumably for political reasons and to regain the Lord Baltimore title. Afterwards, in 1713, he petitioned the crown to restore family control of Maryland, but died in April 1715, before action could be taken.

CHARLES CALVERT, 5TH LORD BALTIMORE – This Charles succeeded to the title following his father's (Benedict's) death in 1715, and the crown restored to him the full proprietary powers the family originally had. He was educated, honest, and good–natured, but weak. In 1732, he went to Maryland to settle with William Penn the dispute that continued over the Maryland–Pennsylvania boundary, and was talked out of 2–1/2 million acres that should have belonged to Maryland. During his proprietorship, the city of Baltimore was founded. Charles lived until 1751.

FREDERICK CALVERT, 6TH LORD BALTIMORE – Charles' son Frederick was a mean degenerate. He had little interest in the colony except for revenue and tax purposes, and to avoid taxes, he even refused to contribute to defense of the colony during the French and Indian Wars. He died in Naples in 1771. He had no legitimate heir, and the title and Calvert proprietorship of Maryland died with him.

BIBLIOGRAPHY

Some of the references used in preparation of this booklet, and related literature that you might find of interest:

Andrews, Matthew Page, *History of Maryland: Province and State*, Tradition Press, Hatboro, PA, 1965

Cochrane, Laura C., et al, *History of Caroline County, Maryland, From Its Beginning*, Regional Publishing Company, Baltimore, 1971

Cozzens, Arthur B., *Whaleyville*, Worcester County Library, Snow Hill, 1972

Delderfield, Eric R., *Kings and Queens of England*, Stein and Day, Inc., New York, 1972

Dozer, Donald Marquand, *Portrait of the Free State*, Tidewater Publishers, Centreville, 1976

Earle, Swepson, *The Chesapeake Bay Country*, Thomsen–Ellis Company, Baltimore, 1934

Earle, Swepson, ed., *Maryland's Colonial Eastern Shore*, Weathervane Books, New York, 1916

Emory, Frederic, *Queen Anne's County, Maryland – Its Early History and Development*, The Maryland Historical Society, Baltimore, 1950

Footner, Hulbert, *Maryland Main and the Eastern Shore*, Tradition Press, Hatboro, PA, 1972. Originally published by Appleton–Century Company, Inc., 1942.

Footner, Hulbert, *Rivers of the Eastern Shore*, Tidewater Publishers, Centreville, 1944

Hall, Clayton Colman, *The Lords Baltimore and the Maryland Palatinate*, 2nd edition, Nunn & Company, Baltimore, 1904

Heyl, Edgar, *I Didn't Know That, an Exhibition of First Happenings in Maryland*, Maryland Historical Society, Baltimore, 1983

Jones, Carleton, *Maryland, A Picture History*, 1632–1976, Bodine & Associates, Baltimore, 1976

Jones, Elias, *New Revised History of Dorchester County*, Maryland, Tidewater Publishers, Cambridge, 1966

Kaminkow, Marion J., *Maryland A to Z*, Magna Carta Book Co., Baltimore, 1985

Kenny, Hamill, *The Placenames of Maryland, Their Origin and Meaning*, Maryland Historical Society, Baltimore, 1984

Mowbray, William W., *The Eastern Shore Baseball League*, Tidewater Publishers, Centreville, 1989

Mullikin, James C., *Ghost Towns of Talbot County*, Easton Publishing Co., Easton, 1961

O'Donnell, James J., *The Counties of Maryland and Baltimore City, Their Origin, Growth and Development*, 1634–1967, State Planning Department, Baltimore, 1968

Papenfuse, Edward C., et al, Maryland, *A New Guide to the Old Line State*, The Johns Hopkins University Press, Baltimore, 1976

Papenfuse, Edward C., and Coale, Joseph M., III, *The Hammond–Harwood House Atlas of Historical Maps of Maryland*, 1608–1908

Preston, Dickson J., *Talbot County – A History*, Tidewater Publishers, Centreville, 1983

Reps, John W., *Tidewater Towns, City Planning in Colonial Virginia and Maryland*, Colonial Williamsburg Foundation, Williamsburg, VA, 1972

Sawin, Nancy C., and Carper, Janice M., *Between the Bays*, The Holly Press, Dover Graphic Associates, Dover, DE, 1978

Sheppeck, Maryl Ellen Mumford, *A History of Ocean City, Maryland*, Eastern Shore Times, Berlin, 1958, 1964

Swann, Don, Jr., *Colonial and Historic Homes of Maryland*, The Johns Hopkins University Press, 1975

Torrence, Clayton, *Old Somerset on the Eastern Shore of Maryland*, Regional Publishing Company, Baltimore, 1966

Truitt, Reginald V., and Les Callette, Millard G., *Worcester County*, Worcester County Historical Society, Snow Hill, 1977

Usilton, Fred G., *History of Kent County, Maryland, 1630–1916*, Perry Publications, Chesterton

Wilson, Woodrow T., *History of Crisfield and Surrounding Areas on Maryland's Eastern Shore*, Gateway Press, Inc., Baltimore, 1977

Wilstach, Paul, *Tidewater, Maryland, Tidewater Publishers*, Cambridge, 1969

INDEX TO THE NAMES